PREVENTING ACTIVIST BURNOUT

A PRACTICAL GUIDE TO STAY COMMITTED, HEALTHY, AND RESILIENT IN YOUR ACTIVISM

DARLENE MEISSNER

ATG

PUBLISHING

Preventing Activist Burnout: A Practical Guide to Stay Committed, Healthy, and Resilient in Your Activism

For information contact : ATG Publishing info@atgpublishing.com - http://www.atgpublishing.com

ISBN: 9781991123145

First Edition: March 2025

10 9 8 7 6 5 4 3 2 1

ADHD
PUBLISHING STANDARDS
—— LEVEL 1 ——

CONTENTS

INTRODUCTION

Activism can be an incredible journey. The energy of a protest, the shared sense of purpose, and the deep belief that you're making a difference can bring immense joy and fulfillment. But behind the powerful images of rallies and inspiring speeches, there are also challenges. Many activists, advocates, and changemakers face exhaustion, chronic stress, and eventually burnout. This quiet struggle affects your ability to create meaningful change and keep up the momentum that activism and advocacy need.

Burnout doesn't happen overnight; it's the result of prolonged and unaddressed stress. It's what happens when passionate people, working tirelessly to change the world, find themselves running on empty. Burnout can make even simple tasks feel overwhelming. Things that used to bring joy and excitement suddenly feel draining and burdensome.

For many activists and advocates, the demands of the cause

often come at the cost of their own well-being, leading to neglected care of oneself, strained relationships, and a sense of isolation. The physical, emotional, and mental toll has the potential to turn passion into frustration, drive into disillusionment, and hope into despair. When activists and advocates reach this point, it can feel like all their efforts are futile, and the once-unstoppable drive to make a difference becomes weighed down by exhaustion and doubt.

I'm writing this book because I've faced these challenges in my personal life and throughout my career. Not only have I suffered due to burnout, but so has my family, my relationships, my ability to complete tasks, and my work performance.

We, as activists and advocates, face unique pressures: work without pay, recognition, or immediate results. We also operate in high-stress environments, opposed by powerful forces and systemic pressures. It is common to feel unsupported by our communities, friends, and even families.

We know the work we do involves long hours, emotional labor, and navigating difficult relationships, often making it feel like an uphill battle. This feeling is compounded when those working alongside us for the same cause sometimes become our worst adversaries, adding an entirely new set of challenges.

The lack of visible progress can weigh heavily, leading to questions like, "Am I really making a difference?" Or "Do I really have what it takes?" These unanswered questions, combined with endless demands, easily lead to burnout. The emotional toll of constantly striving for change, especially when progress is slow or setbacks occur, makes us feel isolated and overwhelmed. We often question our purpose, and without the right support, it's easy for passion to fade into exhaustion.

But it doesn't have to be this way. Burnout can be prevented, and recovering from it is not only possible but essential for both you and the movement. This book is here to help you recognize the signs of burnout, take meaningful steps to prevent it, and find a more sustainable way to keep doing the work you love. It's about helping you continue your important mission while also taking care of yourself, finding joy, and building a strong support network.

Activists and advocates, we have a duty to change the world for the better, but we also have a duty to ourselves: to stay healthy, motivated, and strong. By caring for ourselves, we keep our passion alive and continue to make a real difference. Let's explore how to protect that spark, keep it shining bright, and make the journey as rewarding as the destination.

Part 1: Understanding Activist Burnout

What is Burnout?

Burnout is more than just feeling tired or overworked—it's a state of chronic stress that has profound effects on your body, mind, and emotions. It often begins subtly, with feelings of fatigue or frustration, and then slowly escalates into something more debilitating. It is what happens when prolonged stress goes unaddressed, leaving you feeling emotionally drained, disconnected, and unable to meet the demands of your work and personal life.

In activism, burnout is a particularly common challenge. The emotional labor involved, the sense of responsibility to create change, and the ongoing demands can lead to a state where everything feels like too much. Activists and advocates often start their journey full of enthusiasm and energy, eager to make a difference. But as time goes on, the demands of the work—combined with a lack of tangible results and external support— takes a toll.

Burnout turns your passion into a burden, leaving you disconnected from the cause that once brought you so much purpose.

There are several key signs of burnout to watch for:

Emotional Exhaustion: Feeling drained, overwhelmed, and unable to cope. The emotional highs of activism are replaced by persistent lows, and even small tasks can feel insurmountable.

Cynicism and Detachment: Losing enthusiasm for the work, feeling detached from others, and questioning the value of your contributions. You may find yourself feeling disconnected from your community and less empathetic towards those you are trying to help.

Reduced Performance: Struggling to concentrate, feeling ineffective, or experiencing a decline in your productivity. Tasks that were once easy and enjoyable now feel difficult, making it hard to stay motivated.

Burnout can affect every aspect of your life—physical health, relationships, mental well-being, and the ability to continue activism. It's important to understand that burnout is not a personal failure. It's a natural response to chronic stress, and recognizing it is the first step toward making positive changes.

In the next sections, we'll explore what leads to burnout, how to recognize it early, the stages of burnout, and the steps you can take to prevent it. Activism is vital work, but it doesn't have to come at the cost of your health and happiness. By understanding burnout, you take proactive steps to protect yourself and continue making a difference without sacrificing your well-being.

THE STAGES OF BURNOUT

Burnout is not a sudden event but a gradual process that develops over time. Understanding the stages of burnout helps you identify where you are in the process and take appropriate action.

The five stages of burnout:

Honeymoon Phase: This is the initial stage where you feel enthusiastic, motivated, and passionate about your work. You have high energy levels and are eager to make a difference. During this phase, it's important to establish healthy habits and boundaries to sustain your enthusiasm over the long term. Establishing those healthy habits and boundaries are a lesson we often learn too late. We often don't realize the impact our passion will have on us.

Onset of Stress: As time goes on, the demands of activism start to take a toll. You begin to notice that you're feeling more stressed or overwhelmed. Small signs of stress, such as irritability, anxiety, or difficulty sleeping start to emerge. When you get to this point it is crucial to address stressors otherwise, they will become overwhelming.

Chronic Stress: If the early signs of stress are not addressed, they have the potential to develop into chronic stress. During this stage, stress becomes more persistent, and you start to feel exhausted more often. You will find it hard to focus, experience mood swings, or feel increasingly detached from your work. Looking after yourself—and seeking support are essential during this phase to avoid deeper burnout and maintain your well-being.

Burnout: The symptoms of burnout become more pronounced. Emotional exhaustion, detachment, and a sense of ineffectiveness take hold. Feeling disconnected from your purpose and finding even the simplest tasks insurmountable is a common experience during burnout. It's important to recognize that reaching this stage doesn't mean failure—it's a signal that you need to step back, rest, and seek support to recover.

Habitual Burnout: If burnout is not addressed, it could become a chronic condition. Habitual burnout leads to long-term physical and mental health issues, such as depression, anxiety, and chronic fatigue. At this stage, it's essential to prioritize your well-being, seek professional help if needed, and make significant changes to your lifestyle and approach to activism.

Understanding these stages helps you identify where you may be in the burnout process and take steps to care for yourself before burnout becomes debilitating. In addition, the pressures of our personal lives compound the challenges of fighting for our cause, often intensifying burnout.

Recognizing the signs early and taking action equips you to sustain your activism in a healthy and fulfilling way.

What causes Burnout anyway?

Burnout results from a combination of factors; understanding these is key to preventing it. Some of the most common causes of burnout facing activists and advocates are:

Very Demanding Tasks

Activism involves tackling complex and challenging issues that require significant time, energy, and emotional investment. There are high stakes, tight deadlines, and immense pressure to succeed. Constantly dealing with demanding tasks leads to exhaustion if there isn't enough time for rest and recovery.

Without adequate breaks, the physical and mental toll of managing campaigns, organizing events, and advocating for change quickly leads to burnout. The lack of immediate results, combined with the emotional investment in these demanding tasks, makes the workload feel heavier, adding to the strain.

LACK OF APPROPRIATE SUPPORT

Activists and advocates often operate in environments where emotional and practical support are scarce, making the work even more challenging. The absence of a strong support network can make stress feel unmanageable, leading to isolation and a heightened risk of burnout.

Within the movement itself, a lack of internal support among peers creates additional challenges. Conflicts, competition, and a lack of camaraderie makes activism feel even lonelier, leaving individuals without the collective strength needed to navigate setbacks and celebrate successes together.

It's also important to recognize that emotional support extends beyond the movement. Our personal lives play a significant role in how we manage stress. Balancing activism with the pressures of home life can be overwhelming, especially if we neglect the relationships that sustain us. Prioritizing emotional connections—both within the movement and in our personal circles—is essential to maintaining resilience, staying motivated, and continuing to fight for the causes we care about.

Practical support, such as help with organizing events, managing logistics, or sharing responsibilities, is equally important. When activists and advocates lack this kind of support, they may find themselves overwhelmed by the sheer volume of tasks they need to handle alone. It is common for the lack of appropriate support to lead to a sense of disconnection from the movement, making it harder to stay motivated and resilient in the face of challenges. Building and maintaining a strong support network is essential for sustaining activism over the long term.

LACK OF SELF-AWARENESS

Being unaware of your own stress levels and limits makes it challenging to recognize when to take a break or ask for help. Without self-awareness, it's easy to push yourself too hard and ignore the signs of burnout. Self-awareness means understanding your emotional and physical state, recognizing when you're nearing your limits, and knowing when to step back and take a pause. Having limited self-awareness often leads to breakdowns, highlighting the importance of developing this critical skill.

Many activists and advocates are so focused on the cause that they fail to listen to their bodies and minds, leading to chronic stress and exhaustion.

Developing or building your self-awareness means regularly checking in with yourself, identifying stress triggers, and being honest about how you are feeling. It also involves acknowledging when you need support and being willing to seek it.

Cultivating self-awareness is a critical part of sustainable activism, helping you to recognize when to step back before burnout becomes overwhelming.

No Chance to Take a Break from Everyday Routine

When activism consumes every part of life, it leaves little room for time away from the cause. The sense of urgency that accompanies activist work makes it feel impossible to step back, as there is always another cause, campaign, or crisis that demands attention. However, without the opportunity to disconnect and recharge, stress accumulates, leading to burnout.

Regular breaks are essential for maintaining both mental and physical health. Taking time away from activism helps you gain perspective, process your emotions, and return to the work with renewed energy and focus. Activists and advocates must recognize the importance of rest as part of the long-term strategy for sustainability and resilience in their efforts.

No Satisfaction from Tasks or Work

When activists and advocates do not see progress or feel that their work is making a difference, it leads to a lack of fulfillment. Activism often involves tackling deeply rooted, systemic issues that take years, or even decades, to change. The lack of visible, short-term progress then becomes difficult for activists and advocates to feel that their efforts are worthwhile.

The absence of satisfaction from the work contributes to feelings of hopelessness and burnout, as it becomes challenging to stay motivated without seeing tangible results.

Celebrating small wins and recognizing incremental progress helps, but when these are not evident, the emotional toll is heavy. Activists and advocates feel disillusioned, question their impact, or even become disconnected from the cause they once felt so passionately about. This lack of fulfillment gradually drains energy and enthusiasm, making burnout more likely.

Other Personal Stressors

Personal issues, such as family problems, financial stress, or health concerns, adds to the stress of activism. These additional stressors compound, making it more challenging to manage the demands of activism.

Personal stressors are present to compete for time and energy that would otherwise be devoted to activism, creating a constant juggling act. This leads to feelings of being pulled in multiple directions and struggling to adequately meet all responsibilities. Family issues create emotional strain, financial stress heightens anxiety, and health concerns have the potential to reduce physical stamina—all of which increase the risk of burnout.

The inability to separate personal struggles from activist work creates an overwhelming sense of imbalance, leaving activists and advocates feeling unable to fully focus on either aspect of their lives. Setting boundaries, seeking help, and prioritizing taking care of oneself are essential for effectively managing these intersecting stressors.

LACK OF CONTROL OVER THINGS

Activists and advocates often encounter situations where they have little control over the outcome. Whether navigating bureaucratic systems, confronting entrenched societal attitudes, or facing powerful opposition, the inability to drive change despite significant effort leads to frustration and a sense of helplessness.

This sense of lack of control is particularly challenging in activism because so much of the work is aimed at creating change, and when progress is slow or blocked, it feels like all efforts are futile. Over time, frustration can build up, leading to disillusionment and burnout. It is common for activists and advocates to feel powerless, questioning their abilities and the impact of their work. It is essential to acknowledge that some aspects of activism are beyond individual control and to focus energy on what can be influenced.

Setting small, achievable goals and celebrating incremental progress helps reduce feelings of helplessness and sustain motivation.

WORK-LIFE IMBALANCE

Activism can blur the boundaries between work and personal life, especially when there is a deep emotional connection to the cause. Activists and advocates are often driven by a powerful sense of responsibility, which makes it difficult to step away from their work, even temporarily. The lines between personal time and activism easily become blurred, leading to an "always-on" mentality. This leads to sacrificing hobbies, social relationships, and rest and relaxation—all of which are essential for mental health and well-being.

Without a balance between activism and other aspects of life, it's easy to become overwhelmed and burnt out. The lack of distinction between work and personal life creates a cycle of constant stress, as there is no dedicated time for recovery or taking care of oneself.

Establishing clear boundaries, scheduling personal time, and making a conscious effort to disconnect from activist duties periodically are crucial strategies for preventing burnout and maintaining overall well-being.

LACK OF FAIRNESS

Believe me, I know firsthand how feeling unrecognized or unfairly treated can lead to resentment and emotional exhaustion.

Activists and advocates often put their heart and soul into their work, and when these efforts are overlooked or undervalued, it is incredibly disheartening. The absence of fairness, whether within activist organizations or in the larger social context, contributes to burnout by fostering feelings of frustration and a sense that the work is not appreciated. This lack of recognition leaves activists and advocates feeling invisible or taken for granted, which significantly dampens motivation and morale.

Fair treatment, acknowledgment of contributions, and equitable distribution of responsibilities are crucial for sustaining engagement and preventing burnout. Creating an environment in which every team member feels valued and respected goes a long way in maintaining the emotional health and resilience of activists and advocates.

Recognizing all of the different causes of burnout empowers you to develop effective coping strategies, seek support when needed, and implement healthy boundaries. Taking action not only helps protect your well-being but also ensures that you continue to contribute meaningfully to the causes you care about.

Why Activists and Advocates are at High Risk of Burnout

Activism, by its very nature, demands emotional resilience, dedication, and a willingness to face harsh realities. However, this dedication places activists and advocates at high risk of burnout. Burnout manifests as physical and emotional exhaustion, feelings of helplessness, and disillusionment with the cause they hold dear. To better understand why activists and advocates are particularly vulnerable, it's important to consider several key challenges inherent in this work.

One of the primary reasons for burnout is the emotional intensity of activism. Unlike other professions where emotional detachment is possible, activism frequently requires direct engagement with the harshest realities of human or animal suffering and environmental destruction. Whether activists, advocates, and changemakers are fighting against racial or gender discrimination, advocating for marginalized communities or animal rights, or working to combat climate change, they often witness firsthand the consequences of inequality and injustice. This continuous exposure to trauma often leads to what psychologists' term "secondary traumatic stress", otherwise known as "vicarious trauma." The emotional burden of repeatedly witnessing pain, suffering, and systemic problems accumulates, and if not managed effectively, it leads to exhaustion, hopelessness, and an inability to continue the fight.

Moreover, activism is often marked by a lack of immediate, tangible results. Activists and advocates typically focus on systemic change—a process that commonly takes years, decades, or even a lifetime to achieve. Unlike tasks in more traditional jobs, where one might complete a project and immediately see the outcome, the impact of activist efforts is often less visible and can take much longer to materialize. The absence of immediate results is deeply disheartening. Activists and advocates often spend years working towards a goal, only to face setbacks, public apathy, or outright hostility. This lack of quick wins makes it difficult to sustain motivation, especially in the face of overwhelming issues that seem insurmountable.

Another significant factor is the underappreciation and lack of support that activists and advocates receive. Many activism roles are unpaid or poorly compensated, which adds a layer of financial stress to the emotional challenges. Unlike other professions, activists and advocates may not have access to the resources, support systems, or even respect that are often extended to people working in traditional sectors. Public recognition is often minimal, and this lack of acknowledgment leads to a feeling of isolation. Friends, family, and even the broader community might not fully understand the sacrifices activists and advocates make, and the importance of their work often goes unnoticed. This sense of invisibility fuels burnout, leaving activists and advocates to shoulder the weight of their causes alone, without the appreciation or support they need to stay resilient.

Activists and advocates are vulnerable to burnout because of the confrontational nature of their work. Advocacy often requires directly challenging established norms, systems of power, and entrenched interests. Whether it's protesting against corporations contributing to environmental harm or confronting policies that perpetuate inequality, activists and advocates frequently face resistance from those in power. This opposition comes in many forms—public criticism, harassment, legal threats, physical danger, and even death threats. The constant need to defend their position and justify their actions is draining, and the fear of backlash takes a significant emotional toll.

Additionally, many activists and advocates struggle with setting boundaries. The causes they fight for are deeply personal, blurring the line between work and personal lives. Unlike typical jobs with set hours, activism requires ongoing attention—campaigns, events, social media, fundraising, and educational outreach—all of which demand significant time and energy. Many activists and advocates feel compelled to be available 24/7, answering calls, responding to crises, and managing emergencies. This type of constant, high-intensity engagement leaves little room for taking care of oneself and personal downtime, which is crucial for emotional recovery. Without the ability to step back and recharge, burnout becomes almost inevitable.

The final factor contributing to activist burnout is the profound sense of responsibility many activists and advocates carry. Activism is often driven by the belief that change is not only possible but necessary, and that their efforts are essential to making it happen. This sense of urgency and responsibility, while a powerful motivator, is also a heavy burden. Activists and advocates may feel that taking a break would be tantamount to abandoning the cause or letting down the very people they are trying to help. This internal pressure may prevent activists and advocates from taking the necessary steps to look after themselves, ultimately leading to exhaustion and burnout.

Understanding these challenges is the first step towards addressing burnout. Recognizing that activism is inherently demanding, both emotionally and physically, allows activists and advocates to develop strategies to prioritize well-being. In the chapters ahead, we will delve into ways to build resilience, create boundaries, and cultivate a sustainable approach to activism—one that honours the passion for change without compromising personal health and happiness. By acknowledging the realities of burnout and actively working to mitigate it, activists and advocates can continue their vital work with renewed energy and hope.

RECOGNIZING BURNOUT EARLY

Recognizing burnout early is crucial to preventing it from escalating into something more severe. The sooner you identify the signs, the easier it will be to address them and take action to protect yourself. Early recognition is key to maintaining both your well-being and your ability to continue your activism effectively.

Burnout often creeps in gradually, making it difficult to notice until it has taken a significant toll. To address burnout before it becomes overwhelming, staying attuned to your emotions and physical state is crucial. Here are some early warning signs to look out for:

CONSTANT FATIGUE

Feeling tired even after adequate rest is a clear sign that your stress levels are too high. This goes beyond physical exhaustion; it's emotional fatigue—a weariness that no amount of sleep can fix. It feels like you're constantly running on empty, draining your productivity and darkening your outlook on life. This persistent fatigue is a significant obstacle to staying engaged in the causes you care about, making it essential to address it early.

LOSS OF ENTHUSIASM

When you begin to notice that the activities you once enjoyed now feel like a chore, or if you find it difficult to muster the same excitement and passion for your work, this could be an early sign of burnout. Enthusiasm is often one of the first things to fade when burnout sets in, and it's important to recognize that this loss of passion is a signal that you need a break, rather than a sign that you no longer care about the cause.

DIFFICULTY CONCENTRATING

When stress becomes overwhelming, focusing and thinking clearly become difficult. Tasks take longer than usual, and distractions are harder to ignore. This struggle to concentrate signals that your mental resources are depleted. Your mind might constantly jump from one worry to another, making even simple tasks feel impossible. Recognizing these moments of mental fog is essential for understanding when you need to take time to recharge.

MOOD CHANGES

Burnout causes shifts in your mood, including increased irritability, anxiety, or sadness. You might find yourself becoming more frustrated with people and situations that would not have bothered you before. These mood changes can affect your relationships, making it harder to connect with others or causing unnecessary conflicts. If you notice your patience wearing thin and find yourself snapping at others, it may be time to step back and consider how stress is impacting your emotional health.

NEGLECTING TAKING CARE OF ONESELF

Skipping meals, losing sleep, or neglecting your physical and emotional health are clear red flags that shouldn't be ignored. When stress takes over, taking care of yourself is often the first thing to be sacrificed, however, neglecting it only worsens burnout. Taking care of yourself is crucial for sustaining your energy and resilience and letting go of these routines signals that your well-being is slipping down your list of priorities. Remember, these habits are essential, not optional.

Avoidance and Withdrawal

Feeling overwhelmed leads to avoiding certain tasks or responsibilities altogether. You may find yourself withdrawing from social activities or distancing yourself from friends and family. This withdrawal creates a vicious cycle of isolation, which exacerbates the stress and feelings of burnout. It's important to recognize when you're pulling away from others, as social support is a critical component in managing stress and avoiding burnout.

Acknowledge and Take Action

Recognizing these early signs allows you to take proactive steps to counter burnout before it becomes a major obstacle. It's important to acknowledge these feelings without judgment—burnout is not a weakness, but a sign that you need to take a step back and care for yourself. Taking action early prevents burnout from becoming chronic and difficult to overcome.

If you recognize any of these warning signs, take it as an opportunity to pause and reassess your approach to activism. Ask yourself if you're taking on too much, giving yourself adequate rest, and relying on your support networks when needed. It's important to set realistic boundaries for yourself—it's okay to say no to requests if taking on more will compromise your well-being.

Taking small, proactive steps now helps prevent burnout from worsening and allows you to stay engaged in the long run. These steps include adjusting your workload, scheduling regular breaks, prioritizing sleep, reconnecting with people who support you, and engaging in activities that bring you joy outside of your work. Recognizing that you need rest is not a failure; it's an investment in your ability to continue making a positive impact.

In the following chapters, we will discuss practical strategies for managing stress, building resilience, and creating a healthy balance between your activism and personal life. By recognizing burnout early and taking action, it is possible to continue to contribute to the causes you care about while also safeguarding your health and well-being.

Part 2: Preventing Activist Burnout

ESTABLISHING HEALTHY BOUNDARIES

One of the most effective ways to prevent burnout is by establishing healthy boundaries. Activism is a demanding pursuit, and without clear boundaries, it's easy to overextend yourself, leading to chronic stress and exhaustion. Setting boundaries is not about doing less or being less committed—it's about ensuring that you can sustain your work in the long term by protecting your well-being.

WHY BOUNDARIES MATTER

Boundaries are essential for maintaining a balance between your activism and personal life. When you're deeply invested in a cause, it is challenging to step back, especially when the stakes are high. However, without boundaries, the lines between activism and your personal life blur, making it difficult to rest and recharge.

Healthy boundaries help create space for yourself, allowing you to take breaks, enjoy other aspects of your life, and prevent feelings of resentment or burnout from taking over. Activism is often fueled by passion, but without limits, that passion can turn into exhaustion. By establishing boundaries, you're not only protecting your mental health but also giving yourself the resilience needed to stay engaged and effective in the long run.

IDENTIFYING YOUR LIMITS

The first step in establishing boundaries is to identify your limits. Take some time to reflect on how much time, energy, and emotional bandwidth you have available for activism. Consider your other responsibilities—work, family, friendships, and taking care of yourself —and determine how much time you are able to realistically dedicate to activism without compromising these areas of your life.

It's important to recognize that everyone has different limits, and honouring yours is a crucial part of staying healthy and effective. Some people thrive with many commitments, while others need more downtime to recharge. There's no one-size-fits-all answer—the key is to be honest with yourself about what you can manage. Pushing past your limits might seem noble in the short term, but in the long term, it's a recipe for burnout.

COMMUNICATING BOUNDARIES

Once you've identified your limits, the next step is to communicate them to others. This means clearly communicating with fellow activists and advocates about your availability and setting boundaries when you need time for yourself. It also involves being explicit about which tasks you're willing to take on and delegating those that fall outside your capacity.

Communicating boundaries often feels uncomfortable, especially in a community driven by passion and purpose. However, setting boundaries is essential for maintaining balance and preventing burnout. Remember, saying no when you need to is not a failure—it's a way to protect your ability to contribute in the long term. If you're unsure how to communicate your boundaries, start with small, clear statements like, "I'm available until 6 pm today" or "I need to step back from this project for a week."

When you set clear boundaries, you're modeling healthy behaviour for others in your community. By demonstrating that it's okay to take breaks and say no, you create a culture that respects individual needs and prevents collective burnout.

CREATING A ROUTINE

Another important aspect of establishing boundaries is creating a routine that includes dedicated time for activism as well as time for rest and other activities. Routines create predictability and structure, making it easier to manage your workload and ensure that you have time to recharge.

Whether it's setting aside specific hours each day or week for activism or scheduling regular breaks, having a routine helps you stay on track while preventing the risk of overcommitting. A well-structured routine brings balance—knowing when you'll focus on activism and when you'll focus on other parts of your life reduces anxiety and makes it easier to prioritize taking care of yourself.

Consider creating boundaries around digital engagement. Activists and advocates often find themselves constantly connected—answering emails, scrolling through social media, and staying up to date on the latest developments. While staying informed is crucial, constantly being online drains your energy and creates a sense of urgency that makes it hard to rest. Designate specific times for checking emails and social media and allow yourself to disconnect when needed.

RECOGNIZING AND RESPECTING THE BOUNDARIES OF OTHERS

Boundaries are not just about your own needs; they're also about respecting the needs of others. Recognize that your fellow activists and advocates have limits and be supportive of their need for rest and time away. Just as you want your boundaries respected, it's important to extend that same respect to others.

Encouraging a culture of healthy boundaries within your activist community helps prevent collective burnout and fosters an environment where everyone feels supported and valued. Be mindful of how you communicate with your peers—avoid making assumptions about their availability or pressuring them to take on more than they can handle. Simple acts like checking in with your teammates, asking if they need support, and respecting their decisions goes a long way in creating a positive and sustainable activist community.

PRACTICING SELF-COMPASSION

Establishing and maintaining boundaries is challenging, and there may be times when you feel guilty for stepping back. Practicing self-compassion is crucial during these moments. Remind yourself that taking care of your well-being is a necessary part of effective activism. You can't pour from an empty cup. By prioritizing your health, you ensure that you can continue contributing meaningfully to the causes you care about.

Reframe how you think about rest. Instead of viewing rest as time lost, see it as an investment in your capacity to make an impact. Rest isn't a reward—it's a necessity. Acknowledge the effort you've put in and give yourself permission to take breaks when you need them. Self-compassion means accepting that you are human, with limitations, and recognizing that your value as an activist doesn't come from how much you can do, but from the genuine contributions you make.

Boundaries as a Tool for Sustainable Activism

Boundaries are not barriers to your passion—they are the tools that allow you to continue your work without losing yourself in the process. By establishing and maintaining healthy boundaries, you are able to sustainvism, protect your well-being, and continue to make a positive impact for the long haul. your acti

Consider boundaries as an act of love—both for yourself and for the cause you care about. When you take care of your well-being, you're ensuring that you are present, engaged, and resilient in your activism. This sets an example for others, showing that sustainable activism is about finding balance, honouring limits, and working together to support each other's needs.

Building a Support Network

Activism is a rewarding yet challenging journey; one of the key factors in preventing burnout is building a strong support network. Activism is emotionally and physically demanding and trying to take on the world's problems alone quickly leads to exhaustion. Having a supportive community around you provide the encouragement, resources, and understanding you need to sustain your work long-term.

Why a Support Network is Important

Activism is often portrayed as a solitary pursuit, with individuals standing up against the odds and challenging powerful systems. This imagery creates a false impression that real change is only made by lone heroes. But the truth is, no one can do it alone—and no one should have to. A support network helps navigate the emotional challenges of activism, celebrate victories—no matter how small—and provide comfort during setbacks.

Activism involves dealing with distressing issues, which has the potential to take a toll on your mental health. Knowing that there are people who understand your struggles and genuinely care about your well-being makes all the difference in preventing burnout. A support network reminds you that you're not alone in the fight and that others have your back, helping you persevere when times get tough.

A support network brings diverse perspectives, resources, and skills into the mix. It's easier to find creative solutions to challenges when you are part of a team, rather than trying to figure everything out on your own. Moreover, a support network serves as a safety net, strengthening your resilience in the face of obstacles and setbacks.

Types of Support Networks

There are different types of support networks that can be beneficial for activists and advocates:

Peer Support

Fellow activists and advocates who understand the unique challenges of your work are an invaluable source of empathy, solidarity, and practical advice. Peers can share their own experiences, help you process challenges, and celebrate wins together. Peer support groups, whether in-person or online, provide a valuable resource for staying connected and motivated.

MENTORS

Mentors are individuals who have more experience in activism and offer guidance, support, and perspective. A mentor helps you navigate difficult situations, share the lessons they've learned along the way, and encourage you to keep going. Mentorship is especially helpful when you're feeling stuck or uncertain. Just having someone to turn to who has been in your shoes is incredibly grounding and motivating.

FRIENDS AND FAMILY

While they may not always fully understand the specifics of your activism, friends and family are able to offer emotional support, a listening ear, and a sense of normalcy outside of your activist work. Communicating your needs to those close to you is essential for receiving effective support. While they may not always understand the issues you're fighting for, they care about you and can help you take much-needed breaks when the emotional burden becomes overwhelming.

PROFESSIONAL SUPPORT

Therapy or counseling is often beneficial, as activism involves confronting heavy topics like injustice, trauma, and violence, which take a significant toll on your mental health. A mental health professional has the ability to help you process difficult emotions, develop coping strategies, and maintain your overall well-being. Seeking professional help is not a sign of weakness but rather a proactive way of taking care of yourself so you are able to continue making a difference.

HOW TO BUILD AND MAINTAIN A SUPPORT NETWORK

Building a support network takes time and effort, however, it's an investment in your long-term well-being. Here are some steps you can take to create and maintain a strong support system:

REACH OUT

Don't hesitate to reach out to others. Attend community events, join activist groups, and connect with people who share your values. Building relationships takes time, but putting yourself out there is the first step to finding like-minded individuals who will become part of your support network.

BE OPEN ABOUT YOUR NEEDS

Let others know how they can support you. Whether it's having someone to talk to after a challenging day or requesting help with specific tasks, being open about your needs helps those around you provide the right support. Often people want to help but don't know how—clear communication makes a big difference.

NURTURE RELATIONSHIPS

Support networks are a two-way street. Nurture your relationships by offering support to others while also asking for support when you need it. Being there for your peers not only strengthens your network but also helps create a sense of community and shared purpose. Simple acts of kindness, like checking in on someone or lending a hand when they're struggling, go a long way in building strong bonds.

JOIN SUPPORT GROUPS

Consider joining a support group specifically for activists and advocates. These groups provide a safe space to share experiences, discuss challenges, and find solidarity with others who understand what you're going through. Effective support groups are a source of inspiration, as hearing how others have overcome challenges provides motivation to keep pushing forward.

FIND ONLINE COMMUNITIES

Online communities provide powerful support, especially if local groups aren't accessible. Platforms like social media, forums, and group chats connect you with people worldwide who share your passion for a cause. These communities provide a sense of belonging and shared purpose, and they're often accessible whenever you need them.

THE POWER OF COMMUNITY

One of the most powerful aspects of a support network is the sense of community. Activism sometimes feels isolating, especially when you're faced with opposition or setbacks. Being part of a community reminds you that you're not alone in your efforts. It provides a sense of belonging, shared purpose, and mutual care that helps sustain you through the ups and downs of activism.

Community is a source of resilience. When you're surrounded by people who understand your struggles and share your passion, you gain strength from their support. This collective energy helps you persevere through difficult times, reminding you that you are part of something bigger than yourself. The power of community lies in its ability to amplify individual efforts—together, we are stronger, more effective, and better equipped to face the challenges of the world.

Community fosters accountability. When you have others counting on you, it's easier to stay committed to your cause. Knowing that your fellow activists and advocates are relying on you—just as you rely on them—helps you push through moments of doubt or exhaustion. The bonds you create within a community are a powerful motivator, reminding you that the work you do matters not just for the cause, but for those beside you.

Finally, being part of a supportive community adds joy to the work of activism. The friendships you form, the shared laughter, the camaraderie—these are the elements that make activism sustainable. Celebrating victories, both big and small, with others who understand the effort that went into achieving them is incredibly fulfilling. Joy is an essential part of the journey, and a supportive community helps you embrace and cherish the moments of happiness that make the hard work worthwhile.

Building a strong support network is vital for preventing activist burnout. Activism is a long game and having people by your side who share your passion, support your well-being, and celebrate your victories makes all the difference. Remember, you don't have to do this alone—together, we are stronger, more resilient, and capable of creating lasting change.

BALANCING ACTIVISM AND PERSONAL LIFE

Juggling the demands of activism and personal life often feels like walking a tightrope. The passion that drives you to fight for change is immense, but it also feels overwhelming when the cause consumes every moment of your day.

Just as it's crucial to advocate for systemic change, it is also vital to sustain yourself as an individual. Burnout, exhaustion, and disconnection from loved ones have the potential to undermine the long-term impact you hope to make.

Finding harmony between your activism and personal life requires intentional strategies, self-compassion, and the willingness to pause when needed.

MANAGING TIME AND RESPONSIBILITIES EFFECTIVELY

Effective time management is an essential skill for every activist wanting to balance their responsibilities. It goes beyond simply trying to squeeze more tasks into an already packed schedule. Instead, it's about being intentional with your time—prioritizing tasks in a way that respects both your dedication to change and your need for rest, joy, and well-being. Activists and advocates often find themselves pulled in multiple directions; effective time management allows you to make informed choices that align with your goals and values. It means knowing when to step back, when to push forward, and how to maintain a sustainable pace that allows for long-term impact.

LEARNING TO SAY NO

As an activist, it's easy to fall into the trap of wanting to do everything—attending every protest, organizing every campaign, and supporting every community project. However, saying yes to everything quickly leads to burnout and diminishes your ability to make a meaningful impact. To maximize your contributions, focus on areas where your unique strengths can make the greatest difference, and don't hesitate to say no to tasks that drain your energy or offer limited impact. Saying no isn't a sign of weakness but a strategy to preserve your energy and commitment for the long haul. Recognizing your limits ensures your well-being, which is essential for effective activism. Additionally, saying no creates opportunities for others to step in, share the load, and grow into leadership roles.

CREATING A STRUCTURED SCHEDULE

Set aside specific blocks of time for activism and establish clear boundaries for focusing on yourself. One strategy is to create a daily or weekly routine incorporating dedicated time for rest, relaxation, hobbies, and quality moments with family and friends. By building a rhythm that balances activism with taking care of yourself and your needs, you'll gain a sense of control, reduce stress, and maintain the energy you need to continue making a difference.

Don't forget to schedule regular breaks, allowing yourself time to recharge mentally and physically. Even small, consistent moments of rest make a significant difference in developing resilience. A structured schedule helps you stay organized, avoid last-minute stress, and ensures that your activism efforts are as effective as possible. Consider using tools like calendars, planners, or apps to help you visualize commitments and identify opportunities for rest and balance.

IDENTIFYING PEAK PRODUCTIVITY TIMES

Use these times for your most demanding tasks, whether they are related to activism or personal responsibilities. By aligning tasks with your natural energy levels, you'll be able to work more efficiently and avoid unnecessary exhaustion. Additionally, practicing mindfulness helps you stay present and focused during your activities, whether you're attending a meeting, planning a campaign, or spending time with loved ones. Mindfulness techniques like deep breathing, meditation, and journaling help maintain calm and clarity amid the chaos of activism.

DELEGATION AND COMMUNITY-BUILDING

You don't need to carry the weight of every task on your own shoulders. Activism thrives on community and collective action, so trust in others and share responsibilities. By working collaboratively, you not only lighten your own load but also strengthen the bonds within your activist circle. Distributing tasks helps prevent burnout and empowers others to contribute, ensuring that the movement is sustainable and that no one person is overwhelmed by the workload.

Delegation is not just about efficiency; it is also about community-building. When you delegate, you foster a sense of shared purpose and empower others to take on leadership roles. This collective effort leads to a resilient and adaptable movement. It also means that you are not alone—activism is a team endeavor, and the more people are involved, the stronger and more effective the movement becomes.

Sharing responsibilities allows you to focus on the aspects of activism you are most passionate about, ensuring your contributions are both meaningful and impactful.

By cultivating a culture of collaboration, you create an environment in which everyone feels valued and motivated to contribute. This sense of community is a powerful antidote to burnout, reminding you that you are part of something larger than yourself. When activists and advocates come together, each contributing their unique skills and strengths, the movement becomes not only more effective but also more joyful and sustainable.

FINDING WORK THAT ALIGNS WITH ACTIVIST VALUES

One of the most effective ways to create balance in your life is to align your work with your activist values. When your job reflects the principles that you are passionate about, you are less likely to feel conflicted and more likely to feel fulfilled. This alignment blurs the line between work and activism, allowing your daily efforts to contribute directly to the change you're striving for. When your work supports your values, it reinforces your passion rather than depleting it, making even the most challenging days feel purposeful and worthwhile.

For many activists and advocates, finding work that aligns with their values reduces the emotional and psychological tension that comes with compromising their beliefs. It's important to evaluate job opportunities not just for financial security and career growth, but also for their impact on society. Consider the company's culture, mission, and practices. Does the organization uphold the principles you believe in? Are they making a tangible difference in the areas you care about? Look for organizations that practice what they preach in terms of social, environmental, or community well-being. This makes a significant difference in how you perceive your daily work and its contribution to the greater good.

If a full-time job in a perfectly aligned field is not feasible, consider volunteering or freelance opportunities that allow you to work with values-aligned organizations on the side. Even dedicating a few hours each week to a cause that you care about helps bridge the gap between your career and activism. Volunteering not only supports the causes you believe in but also allows you to connect with like-minded individuals, creating a supportive community that can inspire and sustain your activism.

Remember, finding meaningful work doesn't necessarily mean working directly in a nonprofit or activist role. It could mean choosing a company that operates ethically, works towards sustainability, or supports community engagement. Meaningful work can also involve advocating for positive changes within your existing workplace, such as pushing for environmentally friendly policies or promoting diversity and inclusion initiatives. The goal is to close the gap between your values and your work, so your career feels empowering instead of like a compromise. When your work aligns with your values, it becomes easier to maintain the energy and enthusiasm needed for both your professional life and your activism.

Balancing activism and personal life are ultimately about sustainability—ensuring that your passion for making a difference does not extinguish your joy or energy. It's okay to take a step back, to rest, and to prioritize yourself. Because activism is a marathon, taking care of your well-being is crucial for staying the course. You can only contribute meaningfully to change if you are healthy, fulfilled, and present in your own life.

Remember that taking care of yourself and your needs is not selfish; it is, in fact, a critical part of the resistance, ensuring that your voice remains strong for the long journey ahead. Resting and recharging allows you to bring your best self to the causes you care about, and ultimately, a well-rested activist is a more effective one. Taking care of yourself is a form of resilience, and by caring for yourself, you are caring for the movement and the community around you.

"TAKING CARE OF YOURSELF" AS A PRIORITY

In activism and changemaking, it's easy to lose yourself in the cause, pouring all your energy into the mission while neglecting your own needs. Activism is fueled by passion, but when we run ourselves empty, we're unable to effectively help anyone—including ourselves. Prioritizing taking care of ourselves means understanding that your physical, mental, and emotional health are not luxuries—they're essential.

This isn't about indulging yourself; it's about survival and staying effective. When you give yourself the space to choose what you need—be it rest, support, or simply a moment of peace—you're investing in your ability to make a lasting impact. Sustainable activism is about nurturing your resilience and well-being so you can stay in the fight for the long haul, continuing to make the meaningful difference you set out to achieve.

COMMON TRADITIONAL ACTIVITIES TO TAKE CARE OF YOURSELF

EXERCISE: MOVING YOUR BODY, HEALING YOUR MIND

Exercise is one of the simplest, yet most effective ways to care for yourself. Research has found that engaging in regular physical activity has a profound effect on your mood, stress levels, and energy. Exercise releases endorphins, often referred to as the body's natural "feel-good" chemicals, which help reduce anxiety and improve overall mood. Additionally, it boosts your confidence and sense of accomplishment, particularly when you set and achieve small goals for yourself, such as walking a bit further or trying a new exercise class.

When you're working for change, it's easy to feel overwhelmed. Moving your body helps clear your mind, release tension, and offers a momentary escape from the pressures of advocacy work.

Physical activity has long-term benefits, including improved cardiovascular health, enhanced immunity, and better sleep quality—all of which contribute to your overall resilience. Regular exercise reduces the risk of chronic illnesses including heart disease, diabetes, and high blood pressure. It has a positive impact on mental health by reducing symptoms of depression and anxiety. Exercise does not have to be intense or time-consuming—even a 15-minute stroll in the park, a quick yoga session, or a dance break in your living room can do wonders. The key is to find activities that you genuinely enjoy, making it easier to stay consistent. Consistency is crucial when it comes to reaping the benefits of exercise; moving your body serves as a powerful tool for taking care of yourself and stress relief.

Finding an exercise routine that fits your lifestyle can be a fun journey of self-discovery. The beauty of physical activity is that it can be tailored to your preferences and energy levels. Even on days when you feel drained, gentle stretching or restorative yoga can provide significant benefits without overwhelming your body. Remember, exercise isn't just about physical health; it's about fostering a positive relationship with your body and mind, allowing you to stay energized and focused on your mission.

SLEEP: THE POWER OF REST

Sleep is a cornerstone of physical and mental health which often gets sacrificed when we feel we need more hours in the day to get everything done. Without proper rest, your concentration, decision-making, and emotional resilience suffer. Lack of sleep leads to increased stress levels, weakened immunity, and even long-term health complications such as heart disease or anxiety disorders. Commit to getting enough sleep each night; prioritize it as a non-negotiable part of your routine. Establish a regular sleep schedule by going to bed and waking up at the same time each day, even on weekends.

Establish a bedtime ritual to signal your body that it's time to unwind—examples include reading, meditating, or taking a warm bath. Avoid caffeine and heavy meals before bedtime, as both can disrupt sleep quality. Make your sleep environment as comfortable as possible by keeping the room cool, dark, and quiet. Consider using earplugs or an eye mask if needed and invest in a mattress and pillows that promote restful sleep. Minimize screen time before bed, as blue light interferes with melatonin production, the hormone that regulates sleep.

Proper sleep equips you with the clarity and strength needed to face challenges and make a lasting impact. By embracing sleep as an essential part of your well-being, you not only enhance your own health but also set an example for others in your community, reinforcing the importance of taking care of yourself in the movement for change.

Activism demands creativity and energy, and the foundation of both is a well-rested body and mind. Give yourself permission to rest and understand that rest is a form of resistance against burnout. Rested minds are more adaptable, capable of thinking outside the box, and resilient in the face of setbacks—qualities that are essential for effective activism.

HYDRATION: THE SIMPLE BUT OFTEN FORGOTTEN NEED

Drinking enough water might seem like a minor task, but staying hydrated is essential for your body and brain to function properly. Water plays a critical role in nearly every bodily function, from maintaining body temperature to supporting digestion and nutrient absorption. Proper hydration helps sustain energy levels, improve focus, and regulate mood—all vital qualities for handling demanding work. Without adequate hydration, you may experience fatigue, headaches, or difficulty concentrating, which can significantly hinder your ability to contribute effectively.

Keep a water bottle with you throughout the day, especially during busy stretches, and check in with yourself to see if you're drinking enough. Infusing your water with fresh fruits, herbs, or even a splash of lemon can make hydration more enjoyable. Herbal teas and water-rich foods such as cucumber, watermelon, and oranges help you stay hydrated. It's important to listen to your body's signals—feeling thirsty means you've already waited too long. Make hydration a habit, not an afterthought, and you'll notice the difference in your overall energy and mood.

BALANCED DIET: FUELING YOURSELF WELL

Eating well goes hand in hand with feeling well. When you're juggling a busy schedule, skipping meals or grabbing fast food might seem like an easy solution, but poor nutrition catches up with you. A balanced diet gives you the energy to keep going and helps stabilize your mood. Consider batch-cooking and meal-prepping to ensure you always have healthy options available, especially on those days when time is limited.

A balanced diet includes a variety of foods that provide essential nutrients, such as proteins, healthy fats, complex carbohydrates, vitamins, and minerals. Focus on whole foods like fruits, vegetables, lean proteins, and whole grains, which nourish your body and support optimal health. Avoid relying on processed foods and sugary snacks, which lead to energy crashes and negatively impact your mood. Eating regularly throughout the day helps maintain steady energy levels, preventing irritability or fatigue that often accompanies hunger.

Incorporate mindful eating into your routine by taking the time to savor your meals without distractions. This practice not only helps with digestion but also allows you to fully appreciate the food you're eating, turning mealtime into a moment of taking care of yourself. Proper nutrition is the fuel that keeps you going, and by nourishing your body with high-quality foods, you are able to maintain the stamina needed for the important work you do. Eating well is an investment in your health, and the energy needed to sustain your activism.

MAKING TIME FOR PERSONAL HOBBIES AND ACTIVITIES OUTSIDE OF ACTIVISM

As important as it is to dedicate yourself to a cause, it's equally essential to nurture other aspects of who you are. You are more than your activism. Taking time to engage in hobbies and personal activities not only provides relaxation, but it also brings joy and fulfillment that sometimes feel elusive amidst intense advocacy work. These activities offer moments of personal creativity and expression that are incredibly rejuvenating.

Hobbies are not a luxury; they are an essential part of maintaining your mental health and well-being. Engaging in creative pursuits stimulates different parts of the brain, offering a welcome break from the constant problem-solving and strategizing that activism often requires.

Engaging in hobbies allows you to tap into different aspects of your personality that are not directly related to activism. Hobbies provide a necessary mental shift, giving you a break from the emotionally charged and challenging work you do. They help release pent-up stress and serve as an outlet for emotions that may be difficult to express otherwise. These activities are a reminder that your value isn't solely tied to your productivity or the causes you champion, but also to the unique skills, talents, and passions that make you who you are.

It's important to schedule time for these activities just like you would any other commitment. By setting aside moments for yourself, you allow your mind to decompress, helping you stay focused and passionate about your cause. Moreover, hobbies can be a source of inspiration, sparking new ideas that you can bring back to your activism with fresh perspectives.

Hobbies can serve as a reminder of the beauty and joy in the world, which can be easy to overlook when you're constantly focused on problems that need solving. Whether it's the satisfaction of completing a knitting project, the thrill of capturing the perfect photo, or the calm of tending to a garden, these activities help you appreciate the small moments of happiness that make life meaningful. By cultivating these experiences, you can maintain a positive outlook and stay motivated in your activism, even when faced with setbacks.

Hobbies create opportunities to connect with others outside of the activist community. For example, joining a book club, taking an art class, or participating in a local sports league enables you to form new friendships and expand your support network. These connections can be incredibly enriching, offering a sense of belonging and camaraderie that is separate from your advocacy work. Building relationships with people who share your interests but are not involved in activism provides a refreshing change of pace and helps prevent the isolation that accompanies intense advocacy efforts.

Think of it this way: hobbies and non-activism interests aren't distractions from your mission; they're what make it sustainable. These activities help you stay connected to your sense of self outside of your role as an activist, reminding you that your identity is multifaceted. When you engage in something you love, it brings a sense of balance and perspective, helping to prevent burnout. Hobbies keep you grounded and provide much-needed joy. When you nurture these aspects of yourself, you build emotional resilience, which in turn strengthens your ability to continue your activism without losing sight of who you are.

Ultimately, making time for hobbies and personal activities is about honouring yourself as a whole person. It's about recognizing that your well-being is intertwined with your ability to make an impact. When you allow yourself the time to enjoy life beyond your advocacy work, you create a more balanced, sustainable approach to activism—one that acknowledges the importance of joy, creativity, and personal fulfillment. By investing in your own happiness, you ensure that you can continue to contribute to the causes you care about with energy, passion, and resilience.

EMBRACING THE VALUE OF SELF-DIRECTED FREEDOM

Taking care of yourself isn't selfish. It's an essential practice that allows you to continue your activism effectively, without becoming overwhelmed or burnt out. Remember, you're a human being, not a machine. Taking care of yourself is taking care of the movement, because when you're at your best, you can give your best.

Taking care of yourself involves acknowledging that your health—mental, physical, and emotional—directly impacts the work you do. It's about recognizing the limits of your energy and understanding that rest is a vital component of effective, sustainable action. Prioritize taking care of yourself as a foundational part of the work you do. Embrace exercise, sleep, hydration, good nutrition, and personal hobbies as pillars that hold you up, so you can continue holding up others.

Taking care of yourself means recognizing when you need help and reaching out for support. Building a support network of friends, family, or fellow activists and advocates provides an additional layer of care, allowing you to share your burdens and celebrate your successes. Having people that you trust to lean on during challenging times prevents isolation and can provide fresh perspectives on difficult situations.

Practice setting boundaries to protect your time and energy; say no when you need to. By setting clear boundaries, you ensure that you're not overextending yourself, allowing you to maintain a healthy balance between work and personal life. By taking care of yourself, you model healthy behaviour for others, helping to create a culture of sustainability within the activist community.

Taking care of yourself includes finding ways to celebrate your achievements—big or small. Recognizing and appreciating your efforts, even if the outcome isn't perfect, can boost morale and reinforce your sense of purpose.

Taking time to reflect on successes and challenges is a key part of personal growth, allowing you to adjust your approach when needed and celebrate the progress you've made. Whether it's treating yourself to a favorite meal, taking a day off, or simply spending time with loved ones, these moments of joy and gratitude are crucial for maintaining motivation and passion in your work.

Ultimately, taking care of yourself is about acknowledging your humanity and understanding that you deserve care and compassion just as much as anyone else. It's about giving yourself the grace to rest, breathe, and find joy, so that your passion for change can thrive without consuming you. Embrace taking care of yourself as an ongoing practice, one that evolves with your needs, and know that by doing so, you are making a powerful contribution—not just to your cause, but to yourself and those around you.

By incorporating taking care of yourself into your life, you are investing in your longevity as an activist and ensuring that you can continue to fight for what matters without sacrificing your well-being.

Remember that true change starts from within, and caring for yourself is the first step toward building a more compassionate, sustainable world. When you make taking care of yourself a priority, you not only enhance your own capacity to create change, but you also inspire others to do the same, fostering a movement that is driven by resilience, empathy, and collective strength.

FINDING MEANING BEYOND IMMEDIATE SUCCESS

It's tempting to think that progress is all about quick wins—closing deals, adding accolades, or hitting career milestones. While these short-term successes are motivating, true fulfillment often lies beyond the immediate. It comes from the lasting impact you make, the values you uphold, and the growth experienced over time. It's about creating something that endures, making a difference that goes beyond yourself, and contributing to a larger purpose.

Activism is a long game, and pursuing long-term goals means staying committed, even when the journey is challenging, or the rewards aren't instantly visible. It means finding intrinsic rewards in the process itself—valuing growth, integrity, and the journey of becoming your best self.

Celebrating meaningful small victories along the way helps to keep motivation alive and reminds us that progress is often incremental. These small wins accumulate, each one adding a layer of depth to our understanding of success. Together, they redefine success in a deep, lasting way, shifting the focus from fleeting achievements to a meaningful, purpose-driven journey.

THE VALUE OF LONG-TERM GOALS VERSUS SHORT-TERM WINS

Imagine life as a hike up a mountain range. Each peak offers a moment of exhilaration—a brief view that reassures you of your progress. These moments are valuable; they renew your energy and encourage you to keep going. Short-term wins are like these small peaks—they validate your efforts and push you forward. However, the journey isn't just about reaching individual summits. It's about embracing the entire range—appreciating the difficult climbs, the breathtaking views, and the valleys in between, celebrating the persistence it takes to keep moving.

Long-term goals require us to dig deeper, and to develop a vision that extends beyond the immediate future. These goals come with challenges and setbacks, but it is precisely through these experiences that we grow. They demand resilience, patience, and an understanding that growth is gradual and often unpredictable and provide a sense of purpose that drives us to stay the course even when things get tough.

Balancing the desire for short-term wins with a long-term vision means embracing delayed gratification. It's about understanding that meaningful accomplishments take time and choosing actions today that may not yield immediate results but are essential for your growth. This could include investing in relationships that bring joy and depth to your life, expanding your knowledge through continuous learning, honing your craft even when progress feels slow, or dedicating time to projects that align with your core values. These efforts may not offer instant gratification but lay the groundwork for a more fulfilling future.

The satisfaction of achieving a long-term goal is deeper and more enduring than the fleeting excitement of a quick win. It reflects not only who you are today but also the person you're evolving into—someone willing to invest in what truly matters. Long-term success is about growth, commitment, and staying true to your journey, knowing that each effort moves you closer to the vision you hold for yourself.

It's this patient, unwavering commitment to a larger vision that helps us find fulfillment beyond the temporary thrill of immediate success. Long-term goals teach us that success is not just about the endpoint but also about the resilience and growth we develop throughout the process. When we embrace this mindset, we begin to see that each small effort, each seemingly minor step forward, is a significant part of the greater whole. The journey becomes rich with meaning, filled with opportunities to learn and grow, and become more aligned with our true selves.

RECOGNIZING THE IMPORTANCE OF INTRINSIC VALUE IN ACTIVISM

Finding meaning beyond immediate success starts with recognizing intrinsic value—especially in pursuits like activism that may not bring outward recognition. Activism, whether for social justice, environmental change, animal rights, or community development, is an uphill journey. It's marked by incremental shifts rather than massive, game-changing transformations. The intrinsic value lies in the process: knowing you are part of something that matters, standing up for your beliefs with integrity, and realizing that every effort, no matter how small, contributes to meaningful change. True change takes time, and every contribution, however minor it may seem, is part of a much larger collective effort.

Even when results aren't immediately visible, the act of showing up and staying committed holds deep value. Activism is a marathon, driven by the determination to persist despite slow progress. Along the way, intrinsic value is also found in the relationships you build— with fellow activists and advocates, the community you serve, and yourself as you grow in resilience and understanding.

Activism demands a deep understanding of the

interconnectedness of our actions. The smallest acts often create ripples that extend far beyond what we can see. A conversation that seems insignificant might inspire someone else to take action, ultimately leading to significant change. Recognizing this interconnectedness helps us appreciate the importance of every effort, no matter how small it may seem at the time. When we focus on the intrinsic value of our contributions, we understand that our work is part of something larger—something that may take years, or even generations, to fully materialize.

CELEBRATING SMALL VICTORIES

One of the best ways to find sustained motivation is to celebrate the small victories along the way. These small wins are not just milestones; they are confirmation that we are moving in the right direction. They serve as reminders that progress is being made, even when it feels slow. Celebrating these wins helps to break down the larger, daunting goals into manageable steps, helping the journey to feel achievable and less overwhelming. In the context of long-term goals, these victories are the markers that remind us why we started in the first place, keeping us committed to the journey.

This commitment could involve celebrating a new person joining the cause, a policy change, or even a shift in public discourse. These victories often seem minor compared to the grand vision, but they are essential. They provide fuel to keep going, and they bring joy into the process of change. By celebrating small victories, we acknowledge that progress is rarely linear and that each step, no matter how seemingly insignificant, is an integral part of the bigger picture. Each win adds momentum and strengthens our resolve to continue pushing forward. They help build a culture of positivity and resilience within a movement, making it easier for others to stay engaged and motivated.

Celebrating small victories is equally important in our personal lives. Whether we are working towards a career milestone, a health goal, or personal growth, recognizing these small achievements keeps us engaged and motivated. It's easy to become discouraged when we focus solely on the final destination, especially when it feels far away. However, when we take the time to celebrate the smaller achievements along the way, we create a sense of progress and accomplishment that propels us forward. These moments of celebration serve as checkpoints, allowing us to reflect on how far we've come and appreciate the efforts we've made.

Finding meaning beyond immediate success requires us to look at the bigger picture. It's about understanding that the most valuable achievements often do not come with trophies or applause—they come with the quiet satisfaction of knowing that we're working towards something that truly matters. Celebrating small victories helps maintain a sense of purpose and keeps us aligned with our core values. It allows us to find joy in the process, not just in the outcome. This perspective shift is crucial because it turns the journey into a series of rewarding experiences, rather than a relentless pursuit of an end goal. It's in these small victories that we find moments of fulfillment, moments that remind us why we embarked on the journey in the first place.

Moreover, celebrating small victories fosters a growth mindset. It encourages us to view challenges as opportunities for growth rather than obstacles. Each small success builds our confidence, reinforcing the belief that we are capable of achieving larger goals. This positive reinforcement is vital, especially during times when progress feels slow, or setbacks occur. Focusing on what we have achieved, rather than what is still left to do, cultivates a sense of gratitude and positivity that sustains us through the difficult phases of our journey.

Whether it's in our personal lives, our careers, or in the causes we champion, the most meaningful journeys are those that remind us of our capacity for growth, connection, and impact. In those journeys, the value isn't just in crossing the finish line, but in every small victory along the way. Each of these small victories contributes to the larger narrative of our lives, adding richness and depth to our experiences. They remind us that progress is a collection of moments, each one building on the last, and that true success is found not just in the destination but in the journey itself.

By embracing and celebrating every small win, we find the motivation and inspiration needed to continue moving forward, no matter how challenging the path may be.

This mindset helps you stay connected to your "why." It ensures you appreciate the value of every contribution and remain inspired to continue, knowing that progress is happening—even if it's slower than you'd like. Embracing this perspective makes the pursuit of change more sustainable and deeply rewarding.

REDEFINING SUCCESS AS A JOURNEY, NOT A DESTINATION

The temptation of immediate success will always be present, bringing with it the rush of achievement and social recognition. However, finding true meaning requires expanding your view of success to include the quiet and ongoing journey of growth. This involves embracing long-term goals that shape you as a person and valuing the intrinsic rewards of standing up for what you believe in. True success isn't about collecting achievements—it's about the person you become through your experiences and the difference you make along the way.

Meaningful success is not found at the peak of a mountain but in the climb itself. It lies in the valleys you cross, the companions who journey with you, the setbacks you overcome, and the lessons you learn. By valuing long-term goals, celebrating intrinsic accomplishments, and honouring every step—no matter how small—you discover a deeper fulfillment that extends beyond the fleeting joy of short-term wins. The essence of success is built not at the summit but throughout the journey, in the impact you have on others, and the growth that takes place within you.

The path to success is filled with moments of learning, resilience, and self-discovery. It's about embracing the process and understanding that setbacks are not failures but stepping stones that make you stronger and wiser. Success involves appreciating the people who support you, the challenges that refine you, and the progress you make—even when it isn't immediately visible. Each step, struggle, and triumph become part of a larger narrative that shapes your character and legacy.

Focusing on the journey rather than the destination allows you to see success as a series of meaningful experiences rather than isolated accomplishments. This perspective encourages pride in effort, persistence, and joy in the present moment, rather than constantly chasing the next milestone. Redefining success in this way creates a life filled with purpose, depth, and connection—a life where every step, decision, and action align with your values and contributes to a greater sense of fulfillment.

Ultimately, success is not about accolades or recognition but about the person you've become through your journey. It's about how you've touched others, how you've grown, and how you've stayed true to your values despite challenges. Looking back, you realize that every step, misstep, and moment was worth it—not for what you achieved, but for the meaning you created along the way. Shifting your focus from the outcome to the journey allows you to experience life's richness and find success in every step that brought you there.

PART 3: DEALING WITH BURNOUT

STEPS TO RECOVER FROM BURNOUT

Burnout is a profound state of physical, emotional, and mental exhaustion caused by prolonged stress. The first and most important step in overcoming burnout is acknowledging the problem. Many people, driven by purpose, overlook warning signs and try to "push through," but denial only leads to deeper exhaustion. Recognizing and admitting burnout is not a sign of weakness—it's the first powerful step toward healing.

Once you've acknowledged the issue, seek support. Reach out to friends, family, or professionals who can help lighten the load and provide guidance. Burnout is not something you need to face alone. Sharing your struggle connects you to resources and reminds you that support is always available.

To address burnout, it's crucial to identify the sources of your stress. Reflect on the aspects of your life or work that contribute to exhaustion. Is it an overwhelming workload, unrealistic expectations, or poor boundaries? By pinpointing these factors, you can begin to implement changes like delegating tasks, setting realistic goals, or saying no when necessary. Understanding what caused burnout helps prevent it from recurring.

Developing a consistent routine of taking care of yourself is a cornerstone of recovery. Prioritizing yourself and taking care of yourself isn't about indulgence; it's about practices that support your physical, emotional, and mental well-being. Exercise, mindfulness, spending time with loved ones, and ensuring downtime to relax are all strategies to rebuild resilience and stop burnout from recurring. These practices create a foundation for sustained recovery.

Burnout often stems from blurred lines between personal and professional life, making boundaries essential. Setting boundaries means clearly defining what's acceptable for you and communicating those limits to others. For example, avoid answering work emails during personal time, reduce your workload, and prioritize hobbies that bring you joy. Boundaries help you maintain balance and protect the time you need to recharge.

Recovery doesn't happen overnight, so it's important to celebrate progress along the way. Each step you take—whether it's seeking help, setting boundaries, or feeling a spark of renewed energy—is a victory. By acknowledging these small wins, you remind yourself that recovery is possible. Burnout takes away your sense of power, but every positive step forward helps you reclaim your energy, joy, and sense of purpose.

STRATEGIES FOR REGAINING ENERGY

REST

Rest is the foundation of recovery from burnout. Many people underestimate its importance, often equating it solely with sleep. However, true rest involves stepping back from responsibilities and giving yourself permission to recharge. This might mean scheduling days for comforting activities, disconnecting from stressful environments, or simply allowing yourself to be still. Rest also includes restorative practices such as taking long walks, practicing gentle yoga, or engaging in creative hobbies like painting or journaling. These activities shift your focus away from stress, helping your mind and body unwind.

Prioritizing quality sleep is another essential component of rest.

Restful sleep is crucial for both emotional and physical health, and establishing a sleep routine can significantly impact your recovery. To improve sleep quality, set a consistent bedtime, invest in a comfortable mattress and pillow, minimize screen time before bed, and create a calming sleep environment. Relaxation techniques like deep breathing or guided meditations before bed can further enhance your ability to rest deeply.

Mental rest is equally important. This involves giving your mind a break from the constant demands of work and responsibilities. Mental rest might include spending time in nature, practicing mindfulness, or engaging in low-effort activities that allow your thoughts to settle. It's about releasing the pressure to be productive every moment and recognizing the value of stillness.

True rest requires intentionality and the understanding that it is essential—not indulgent. It is not a luxury but a necessity when recovering from burnout, allowing you to restore your energy and resilience. By embracing rest in all its forms—physical, mental, and emotional—you create the foundation needed for healing and growth.

FINDING JOY AND MOTIVATION AGAIN

When you're burnt out, it's easy to lose sight of what once

brought you happiness and fulfillment. To move forward, it's important to reignite your passion in a sustainable way that allows you to continue your work without draining yourself. Start by revisiting the activities and values that initially inspired you. Take time to evaluate your current approach—ask yourself if it's sustainable or if adjustments could make it more rewarding and less taxing.

One way to reignite your passion is to redefine success. When you're burnt out, your previous definitions of success may no longer serve you. Adjust your expectations and goals to fit your current needs and capacity. This could mean focusing on smaller, attainable achievements or finding fulfillment in aspects of your work that genuinely bring you joy. Redefining success removes unnecessary pressure and allows you to find motivation in a way that aligns with your well-being.

Reconnect with your community to rediscover your sense of purpose. Burnout often brings a sense of isolation, but engaging with like-minded individuals can remind you that you're not alone. Join local groups related to your interests, attend workshops, or participate in online communities where people share similar goals and challenges. The support and camaraderie of a community can be incredibly motivating and help restore your enthusiasm for your work.

Engage in creative pursuits to find joy and release stress.

Creativity allows you to express yourself freely and reconnect with a sense of playfulness and curiosity, which are often lost during burnout. These activities can rejuvenate your spirit and help you rediscover joy.

Develop meaningful rituals that reinforce your moral convictions. Engage in small practices that remind you of why you started—read about inspiring figures, spend time in nature, or meditate on your mission. Journaling is a powerful tool for reflection. Writing about your thoughts and experiences helps you process emotions, track progress, celebrate wins, and identify patterns that contribute to both burnout and recovery.

Lastly, celebrate progress, no matter how small. Finding motivation after burnout is a gradual process, and each milestone is worth acknowledging. Every step forward is a testament to your resilience; recognizing these moments fosters a renewed sense of purpose and joy. Celebrating progress not only boosts motivation but also reinforces the belief that recovery is possible and worthwhile.

THERAPY AND PROFESSIONAL SUPPORT

When burnout becomes overwhelming, therapy and professional support provide an essential lifeline. A professional therapist helps you navigate the underlying factors contributing to burnout and works with you to develop effective coping strategies. Therapy offers a safe space to explore the emotions, beliefs, and behaviours that exacerbate burnout. Therapists equip you with personalized tools for stress management, assist in setting realistic goals, and guide you in improving work-life balance. Cognitive-behavioral therapy (CBT), for example, is particularly effective in helping individuals reframe negative thought patterns contributing to burnout.

If therapy feels financially out of reach, there are affordable and free mental health resources available. Community clinics, support groups, and online platforms offer assistance without significant financial burden. Many platforms provide sliding-scale fees based on income, and some therapists offer reduced rates for those in financial need. Additionally, mental health organizations often provide free or low-cost counseling services. Exploring employee assistance programs (EAPs) through your workplace is another option, as they often include short-term counseling and mental health resources at no cost.

As we talked about earlier in the book, support groups are another invaluable resource. Talking with others who have experienced similar challenges fosters a sense of community and understanding. These groups remind you that you are not alone and provide encouragement and shared experiences. Support groups are widely available both in person and online, making them accessible regardless of location or schedule.

Coaching is an option for addressing burnout. Professionals specializing in stress management and resilience can help you set actionable goals, build coping skills, and develop strategies to prevent burnout in the future. Unlike therapy, coaching focuses on practical, forward-thinking strategies and is often goal-oriented, making it an excellent complement to therapeutic interventions.

Seeking professional help is an investment in yourself and a crucial step toward recovery. Reaching out for support is not a sign of failure, but a courageous and proactive choice. With the right resources, you are able to rebuild your mental well-being, and regain confidence, allowing you to move forward with renewed strength and purpose.

PART 4: COLLECTIVE APPROACHES TO PREVENT BURNOUT

Creating Supportive Structures in Activist Communities

Burnout is a common risk in activist circles, making supportive structures essential for sustaining social change. To foster resilience, activist communities must prioritize mutual support as a core value. One effective approach is developing formal support groups, which offer dedicated spaces for members to share experiences, voice concerns, and receive validation. These groups turn vulnerability into collective strength, transforming it from a personal burden into a shared source of empowerment.

Support groups take many forms, such as peer-led sessions, facilitated workshops, or online communities. These gatherings are not only about sharing struggles but also celebrating successes, however small they may be. By acknowledging both positive and negative emotions, members feel seen and heard, reducing isolation and fostering a sense of belonging. Support groups provide opportunities for collective problem-solving, where members draw on their experiences to find creative solutions. Skill-building sessions, such as conflict resolution, time management, and stress management workshops, further empower individuals to navigate challenges and prevent burnout.

Mentorship is another cornerstone of supportive structures. Experienced activists and advocates are able to guide newer members, easing the onboarding process while sharing valuable knowledge and strategies. Mentorship is a reciprocal relationship; while mentors offer insights and support, they also gain fresh perspectives and renewed inspiration. Mentorship can be formalized through structured pairings or develop organically through community interactions. It is often tied to specific projects or campaigns, enabling hands-on collaboration that strengthens bonds and accelerates learning. By fostering mentorship, activist communities create a culture of learning and mutual growth.

Non-work-related gatherings, such as potluck dinners, art workshops, or nature hikes, give activists and advocates a chance to unwind and build relationships outside the pressures of their work. These moments of joy and playfulness remind the community that rest and connection are vital components of sustainable activism. Incorporating wellness-focused events—such as yoga classes, meditation sessions, or group fitness activities—adds another layer of support by promoting both mental and physical health. For deeper restoration and camaraderie, retreats or weekend getaways provide immersive opportunities to recharge while strengthening bonds within the community.

Effective communication is essential for building cohesion within activist communities. Clear communication channels, such as group chats, online forums, or newsletters, keep members informed about opportunities to connect and share resources. Active listening is equally important—creating safe spaces where individuals feel heard without judgment builds trust and solidarity. Regular check-ins, whether one-on-one or in groups, allow members to share how they're feeling and what they need, ensuring the community adapts to prioritize well-being.

Addressing the emotional toll of activism is crucial. Trauma-informed care acknowledges the impact of trauma and provides appropriate support, such as mental health workshops or counseling. Training members to recognize signs of burnout and emotional distress equips the community to respond proactively, fostering a safe, nurturing environment.

Celebrating achievements, both big and small, is vital for morale. From a simple shout-out during a meeting to an event celebrating a campaign's success, recognizing members' contributions reinforces their sense of value. Celebrations offer moments to pause, reflect, and appreciate progress, which boosts motivation and energy for the long haul.

Bringing together formal support groups, mentorship, collective activities, open communication, trauma-informed care, and regular celebrations helps create a well-rounded support system. This approach puts individual well-being first, builds resilience, and reduces burnout. By fostering this kind of environment, communities can stay strong and keep driving meaningful social change for the long haul.

Shared Responsibility and Avoiding Overcommitment

Shared responsibility is a fundamental principle for preventing burnout. Activism involves a wide range of tasks, from organizing events and managing logistics to handling communications and providing emotional support. When a small number of individuals take on too many responsibilities, they quickly become overwhelmed, which leads to burnout. To ensure that the workload is distributed evenly and sustainably, it is crucial to create a culture that values delegation and shared effort.

How to Delegate Within Activist Groups

Delegation is essential for maintaining a healthy balance of responsibilities. It involves assigning tasks based on individuals' strengths, interests, and availability, ensuring no one is overburdened. Effective delegation begins with identifying the tasks that need to be completed and breaking them into manageable parts. Once tasks are clearly defined, group members can volunteer for roles that align with their skills and interests. This approach not only prevents overcommitment but also allows individuals to contribute in ways that are personally fulfilling.

To make delegation effective, clear processes and tools are crucial. Establish systems for assigning and tracking tasks, such as spreadsheets, project management software, or task boards, to keep everyone aligned. Regular check-ins ensure tasks are progressing smoothly and provide opportunities for members to ask for support. Delegation isn't just about assigning responsibilities; it's about fostering an environment where individuals feel comfortable seeking help and roles can be adjusted to accommodate changes in capacity.

Transparency and open communication are key to successful delegation. Everyone should understand what needs to be done, who is responsible for each task, and when tasks are due. This prevents misunderstandings, ensures tasks are completed on time, and builds trust within the group. Transparency allows members to see how responsibilities are distributed and gives them the chance to step in when someone is struggling.

Rotating leadership roles is equally important for preventing burnout and fostering growth. Periodic rotation ensures that knowledge and skills are shared across the group, preventing any one person from becoming overwhelmed by leadership demands. It allows members to gain experience in various aspects of organizing, strengthening the group as a whole. By sharing leadership responsibilities, the group cultivates a sense of collective ownership and accountability, where all members can contribute to the group's success.

Rotating leadership broadens perspectives and keeps the group dynamic. Each leader brings unique ideas, skills, and approaches, ensuring adaptability and fresh thinking. Rotation also provides individuals with opportunities to develop new skills and build confidence—essential for long-term sustainability in activist communities. This practice nurtures a culture of empowerment and mutual support, ensuring leadership remains accessible to everyone rather than limited to a select few.

Importance of Each Person Focusing on Their Strengths to Create Balance

Activist groups are made up of people with diverse skills, experiences, and strengths. Encouraging individuals to focus on their strengths creates a balanced and effective approach to the work. When people contribute in ways aligned with their skills and passions, they are more likely to feel energized and motivated, helping to prevent burnout. For example, someone who excels at public speaking might take on the role of spokesperson, while another with organizational skills could focus on logistics and event planning.

Not everyone needs to be involved in every aspect of the work. Creating a culture that values specialization allows individuals to focus on specific areas without feeling pressure to do it all. This approach benefits the group by fostering expertise while also giving members a sense of purpose and fulfillment. Specialization ensures that each person can develop their strengths and contribute meaningfully, which enhances the group's overall effectiveness.

Focusing on strengths builds a cohesive and motivated team. When individuals contribute in ways that feel rewarding, it fosters pride and ownership in the work. This sense of ownership is critical for maintaining long-term motivation and engagement. A positive group culture is created when everyone's contributions are recognized and valued, strengthening bonds between members and reinforcing a shared sense of purpose.

As campaigns or projects evolve, roles may need to shift. Balancing responsibilities effectively requires flexibility and open communication. Regular discussions about workload and capacity help ensure that contributions remain manageable and rewarding. Flexibility is key to adapting to the unpredictable nature of activist work. Being open to new responsibilities, stepping back when necessary, and redistributing tasks when someone is overburdened creates a sustainable and supportive environment.

Shared responsibility goes beyond dividing tasks—it fosters trust, support, and solidarity. When everyone feels their contributions are valued and they're not carrying the weight of the work alone, the group becomes more resilient. Shared responsibility strengthens morale, especially during challenging times, by reinforcing a sense of collective purpose. Members are reminded that they are part of something larger than themselves and that their efforts, no matter how small, make a difference.

Maintaining a culture of shared responsibility requires mindfulness and proactive support. Regular check-ins and open conversations about workload, capacity, and well-being are essential. Offering support when someone is struggling and addressing overcommitment helps ensure that everyone is working within their limits. This proactivity creates a sustainable environment where members feel supported and valued.

By embracing shared responsibility, effective delegation, and valuing individual strengths, activist communities can achieve their goals while nurturing their members. This approach ensures that the work remains sustainable, members stay engaged and energized, and the community as a whole remains resilient in the face of challenges. Shared responsibility is not just a strategy for preventing burnout—it's a core principle for building a strong, cohesive, and enduring activist group.

Encouraging Sustainable Activist Practices

Sustainable activism is essential for long-term impact. Activist work is demanding, and without a focus on sustainability, individuals can quickly become exhausted and disillusioned. Encouraging sustainable activist practices means making well-being a core value of the culture. Sustainable activism is about integrating rest, boundaries, and taking care of yourself into the very fabric of activist work.

To achieve sustainable activism, communities must foster a culture that emphasizes balance and recognizes that long-term success depends on the health and well-being of its members. Sustainable activism is not just about preventing burnout; it is about creating an environment where activists and advocates thrive and where their efforts can be sustained over time. This requires a shift in the way we think about activism, from a focus on constant urgency and sacrifice to one that prioritizes resilience, support, and collective care.

One key aspect of sustainable activism is recognizing the importance of pacing. The work is often characterized by intense periods of action; however, it is vital to balance this with rest and reflection. By creating a rhythm that allows for both action and recuperation, activists and advocates are able to maintain their energy and passion for the cause. This might involve planning campaigns in a way that includes downtime or alternating between high-intensity activities and ore restorative tasks. Sustainable activism is about understanding that the work will never be finished overnight and that taking time to rest is a necessary part of achieving long-term goals.

Fostering a sense of shared responsibility is vital. It's our world. We're in this together. When everyone in a group feels responsible for the well-being of their fellow members, a culture of care and support is created. This means checking in on one another, offering help when others are struggling, and being willing to step back when needed. Shared responsibility extends to ensuring that tasks are distributed in a way that respects each person's capacity and well-being. By fostering a culture in which everyone looks out for one another, activist communities are able to create a strong foundation for sustainable action.

Activist work is unpredictable, and the ability to adapt to

changing circumstances is crucial for long-term success. There needs to be a willingness to adjust goals, timelines, and strategies and recognize that flexibility is key to maintaining momentum. Activist communities should encourage their members to be open to change and to see adaptability as a strength rather than a sign of weakness. By fostering a culture that values flexibility, communities are able to better respond to challenges and ensure that their work remains effective and sustainable.

MAKING REST AND WELL-BEING A CORE VALUE OF ACTIVIST CULTURE

Rest is not a luxury; it is a necessity. Activists and advocates often feel pressured to be constantly working, especially when the issues they are addressing are urgent and critical.

Note: *BURNOUT ONLY SERVES TO WEAKEN THE MOVEMENT*

One way to make rest a core value is to build rest into the structure of activist work. Ways to achieve this include setting limits on the number of hours members are expected to work each week, encouraging regular breaks, and allowing time off when needed. Meetings could include designated times for rest or relaxation exercises, such as guided breathing or stretching. By making rest an intentional part of activism, communities send a clear message that well-being is just as important as the work itself.

Set boundaries around availability. Activists and advocates often feel the need to be constantly available in order to respond to crises or take on new tasks. However, this constant availability is unsustainable and leads to burnout. Encouraging members to set clear boundaries around their time—such as not answering emails after a certain hour or taking weekends off—helps protect well-being and ensures they have the energy to continue the work in the long term. Leadership should model these boundaries, demonstrating that it is acceptable and necessary to take breaks and prioritize taking care of yourself.

Creating a culture that values well-being means providing resources and opportunities for taking good care of yourself. Organizing workshops on stress management, offering access to mental health services, or providing spaces for relaxation and reflection are all examples of this. Taking care of your needs is often seen as an individual responsibility, but within activist communities, it should be a collective effort. By providing resources and encouraging open conversations about well-being, an environment is created in which taking care of yourself is normalized and supported.

Celebrate rest and well-being as acts of resistance. The idea that rest is a form of resistance is particularly powerful in the context of activism; individuals are often fighting against systems that devalue their humanity. Resting and taking care of oneself asserts the right to exist and thrive. By framing rest as a radical act, communities shift the culture away from one of constant urgency towards one that values sustainability and long-term impact.

A sustainable activist culture involves recognizing the signs of burnout and taking proactive steps to address it. Encourage members to look out for one another and to speak up if they notice signs of burnout in themselves or others, such as fatigue, irritability, feelings of hopelessness, or a lack of motivation. Creating a culture where it is safe to acknowledge and address burnout, enables communities to take steps to prevent burnout before it becomes overwhelming. This could mean redistributing tasks, offering additional support, or encouraging someone to take a break.

Furthermore, sustainable activism means embracing the idea of collective care. Collective care goes beyond individual self-care and focuses on the ways in which the community can support the well-being of its members. This can include sharing responsibilities, checking in on each other regularly, and creating an environment where people feel comfortable asking for help. Collective care acknowledges that the well-being of each individual is connected to the well-being of the group as a whole. By fostering a culture of collective care, a strong support network that helps sustain the work over the long term is created.

Incorporating rest, boundaries, and collective care not only helps prevent burnout but also makes the work more effective. When activists and advocates are well-rested and supported, they are more creative, more resilient, and better able to respond to challenges. By making rest and well-being core values, activist communities build a foundation for long-lasting, impactful social change.

PART 5: BRINGING IT ALL TOGETHER

What Have We Covered So Far?

As we reach the end of this book, let's take a moment to revisit the key points we've explored on this journey of understanding and preventing activist burnout. We started by defining burnout and examining the unique challenges activists and advocates face—from the emotional intensity of the work to the lack of immediate rewards and support. Activists and advocates work tirelessly, driven by a deep passion for their cause, however, this passion has the potential to lead to exhaustion when not managed properly. We explored how the emotional toll of facing resistance, lack of progress, and feeling unsupported contributes to burnout. Understanding these challenges allows us to develop compassion toward ourselves and recognize the need for proactive measures to prevent burnout.

We learned to recognize the early signs of burnout, such as fatigue, mood changes, and neglecting taking care of yourself, which are crucial to catching burnout before it becomes overwhelming. Fatigue manifests not just physically but also emotionally, making it difficult to find joy in the work that once inspired us. Mood changes, like irritability or feelings of hopelessness, may signal that your emotional reserves are running low. Neglecting your own needs is a significant red flag, placing ourselves at risk of burnout. Recognizing these signs early on is essential for taking action before burnout takes a greater toll on our health and effectiveness as activists and advocates.

We then discussed practical strategies for establishing healthy boundaries, building strong support networks, and balancing activism with personal life. With these tools, we are able to sustain our efforts over the long term without sacrificing our well-being. Establishing healthy boundaries means learning to say no when necessary and understanding that our capacity to contribute is not limitless. By clearly defining when and how we engage in activism, we protect our energy and prevent overcommitment. Building strong support networks is equally important—having peers, mentors, friends, and family to lean on provides emotional support, guidance, and a sense of community. Activism can be isolating, especially when facing resistance; knowing we are not alone in our journey makes it easier to persevere.

Balancing activism with personal life is a key aspect of preventing burnout. Activism is demanding, but it should not come at the expense of our relationships, hobbies, and personal fulfillment. By integrating activism into a well-rounded life, we ensure that we remain passionate and effective advocates for our cause without losing ourselves in the process.

The importance of finding intrinsic value in the work was emphasized, celebrating small victories, and focusing on long-term goals rather than immediate success. These approaches help activists and advocates stay motivated, even when the path is challenging. Finding intrinsic value means connecting deeply with the reasons we chose to become activists and advocates in the first place—understanding that every small action contributes to a greater movement. Celebrating small victories helps us acknowledge progress, even when the ultimate goal feels far away. Focusing on long-term goals allows us to remain resilient in the face of setbacks.

We explored the role of taking care of yourself in preventing burnout. From exercise and sleep, to hobbies and nutrition and hydration, taking care of oneself is a necessity. Exercise releases stress and maintains physical health, while sleep is essential for mental clarity and emotional stability. Engaging in hobbies allows us to express creativity and experience joy outside of activism, which is vital for maintaining our overall well-being. Hydration and nutrition are fundamental aspects of taking care of your needs that are often overlooked when we are busy. The journey to creating change is long and unpredictable, and by taking care of ourselves we can ensure that our passion remains a source of strength rather than a burden.

By making yourself a priority, we create a foundation that supports both our individual health and the collective power of the movement.

Taking Care of Yourself as an Integral Part of Activism

Taking care of your own needs is about understanding that we deserve moments of joy and peace amidst our activist endeavors. Often, activists and advocates become so focused on the cause that they forget to experience the simple pleasures of life—whether it's enjoying a meal with loved ones, spending time in nature, or indulging in a hobby that brings happiness. Joy is a form of resistance in itself. By nurturing joy, we create a positive energy that fuels us to keep going. Allowing ourselves time for laughter, relaxation, and connection is essential for maintaining a healthy perspective. These moments help us remember why we fight for change—to create a world where everyone can live with dignity, fulfillment, and peace.

Activism is emotionally taxing, and it's natural to experience feelings of frustration, sadness, anger, or even hopelessness. Instead of suppressing these emotions, taking care of yourself invites us to honour and process emotions and seek comfort when needed. This could mean journaling, speaking with a trusted friend, or seeking professional counseling. Addressing our emotions helps prevent them from festering and leading to burnout. Acknowledging our struggles does not make us weak; it makes us human. When we care for our emotional health, we build resilience that enables us to face challenges with greater strength and clarity.

While taking care of yourself focuses on individual practices, caring for one another emphasizes the importance of collective care and support. Activism is a collective endeavor; caring for one another is part of what makes movements sustainable. This takes many forms, such as offering practical assistance, emotional support, or simply checking in on fellow activists and advocates. By creating networks of care, we ensure that everyone has the support they need to thrive. We can create buddy systems, form peer support groups, and make space for open conversations about mental health within our activist circles. When we care for each other, we cultivate a culture of compassion and solidarity that strengthens our movement as a whole.

Self-compassion is also a key aspect of taking care of yourself. Activists and advocates often hold themselves to high standards and feel guilty for not doing enough. However, it's important to remember that we are all doing the best we can with the resources we have. Self-compassion means treating ourselves with the same kindness and understanding that we would offer a friend. It means recognizing that setbacks are part of the journey and that it's okay to take breaks when we need them. By practicing self-compassion, we let go of unrealistic expectations and allow ourselves the grace to rest, recover, and grow. This not only benefits our own well-being but also enhances our capacity to contribute effectively to the movement.

Restorative practices are important. Activities like meditation, yoga, deep breathing, and spending time in nature enable us to reconnect with ourselves and find a sense of inner calm. These practices allow us to reflect, slow down, and recharge. For example, meditation quiets the mind and alleviates stress, while yoga releases physical tension and promotes relaxation. Spending time in nature has been shown to improve mood, reduce anxiety, and enhance overall well-being.

While these restorative practices are powerful tools for maintaining balance, traditional approaches such as meditation and yoga may not resonate with everyone. Some may prefer hiking a mountain, going white water rafting, or spending a day at the beach relaxing. Each person has their own way of being restored, and it's essential to honour that. By embracing any practices—whatever they may be—creating moments of stillness and reflection help us stay grounded and focused.

Celebrate achievements, both big and small. Activism often feels like an uphill battle, with progress coming in small increments. By taking the time to acknowledge and celebrate our accomplishments, we create positive reinforcement that keeps us motivated.

Celebrating achievements is as simple as sharing success with a friend, treating ourselves to something we enjoy, or taking a moment to reflect on the impact we've made. These celebrations are important reminders that our efforts matter, helping us stay connected to the purpose behind our work. By recognizing the value of our contributions, we maintain a sense of fulfillment and joy that sustains us through the challenges of activism.

Ultimately, taking care of yourself and your needs is about creating a holistic approach that nurtures our physical, emotional, and mental well-being. It's about understanding that we cannot pour from an empty cup, and that by taking care of ourselves, we are better equipped to care for others and the causes we fight for. Taking care of yourself is not a one-size-fits-all practice; it's a personal journey that requires us to listen to our own needs and respond with compassion. Whether it's through exercise, rest, creative expression, emotional support, or community care, taking care of yourself is the foundation that allows us to thrive.

By making taking care of your needs an integral part of our activism, we ensure that we continue to show up, speak out, and make a difference—sustainably and joyfully.

CREATING A SUSTAINABLE MOVEMENT FOR ACTIVISTS, ADVOCATES AND THE CAUSE

Creating a sustainable movement also involves fostering emotional resilience and establishing mechanisms for dealing with activist fatigue. The emotional burden that comes with advocating for social justice is often immense. Activists and advocates face setbacks, criticism, and resistance, which leads to disillusionment and burnout. Therefore, it is crucial to provide spaces where activists and advocates can express their emotions freely and find support. Emotional resilience is not about suppressing emotions but rather about acknowledging them, understanding their impact, and finding ways to cope constructively. Support groups, regular check-ins, and dedicated time for emotional processing build resilience and support mental health.

Additionally, establishing clear roles and responsibilities within the movement is key to preventing burnout and ensuring that everyone's contributions are balanced. When roles are clearly defined, activists and advocates are left to focus on specific tasks without feeling overwhelmed by the entirety of the movement's demands. This approach reduces stress and creates a sense of purpose and ownership. Role rotation is beneficial, allowing activists and advocates to gain new skills and perspectives while avoiding monotony. By sharing responsibilities and giving activists and advocates opportunities to take on different roles, we build a versatile and engaged community that is better equipped to tackle challenges.

Sustainable activism requires strategic planning and goal setting. By setting realistic, achievable goals, we are able to maintain motivation and avoid the frustration that often comes with trying to tackle everything at once. Breaking down larger objectives into small, manageable tasks creates a sense of progress and accomplishment. Celebrating each milestone, no matter how small, reinforces the importance of incremental change and boosts morale.

Flexibility is crucial—by remaining adaptable, we can respond effectively to changing circumstances and continue to move forward.

To create a sustainable movement, it is important to build alliances and partnerships with other organizations and communities. Collaboration amplifies impact and allows for the sharing of resources, knowledge, and skills. By working together with other groups that share similar goals, we create a broad, powerful coalition for change. Partnerships provide emotional and logistical support, helping to share the burden of activism. By leveraging the strengths of multiple organizations, we increase our collective capacity to address complex social issues and create lasting change. Building strong alliances create a sense of unity and solidarity, reminding activists and advocates that they are part of a larger, interconnected effort for justice.

Keep the movement intergenerational by encouraging mentorship. When young and experienced activists and advocates come together, fresh ideas and energy meet wisdom and experience. Young activists and advocates bring innovative thinking and new approaches, while seasoned activists and advocates offer context and guidance from their years of work. Bridging the gap between generations creates a movement that's both forward-thinking and grounded. Mentorship helps ensure valuable knowledge is shared and the movement stays strong over time.

It is vital to address systemic barriers that contribute to activist burnout. Advocating for better funding, creating resource-sharing networks, and challenging negative stereotypes about activism are all ways to address these systemic issues. By working to remove these barriers, an environment is created in which activists and advocates are supported and able to focus on their work without unnecessary stress.

Financial sustainability is particularly important. Movements that rely solely on volunteer efforts can quickly become unsustainable. Seeking grants, crowdfunding, and building relationships with supportive donors ensure that activists and advocates are compensated for their time and labour, making the movement more equitable and viable in the long term.

A sustainable movement must be rooted in self-reflection and continuous learning. Activism is a learning journey, and movements must be willing to adapt and grow in response to new information and changing circumstances. Regular reflection allows activists and advocates to assess what is working well, what needs improvement, and how the movement can evolve. This process of self-assessment prevents stagnation and ensures that the movement remains responsive to the needs of both the cause and the people involved.

Continuous learning, through workshops, training sessions, and open discussions, also helps activists and advocates stay informed, build new skills, and strengthen their advocacy efforts. Fostering a culture of learning empowers activists and advocates to be more effective in their work and resilient in the face of challenges.

Fostering joy and creativity within the movement is essential for sustainability. Activism is exhausting; therefore, it is important to create opportunities for joy, celebration, and creative expression.

Joy is not a distraction from the work—it is a necessary part of it. By making space for joy, we remind ourselves of the world we are striving to create: one where everyone experiences happiness, fulfillment, and community. Creativity plays a role in problem-solving and helps bring fresh perspectives to the challenges we face. By nurturing creativity, we keep the movement vibrant and adaptable.

To close, building a sustainable movement requires a commitment to both the cause and the well-being of the activists and advocates who drive it. By fostering a culture of care, collaboration, and inclusivity, we create an environment in which everyone feels supported and valued. This not only strengthens our ability to achieve meaningful change but also ensures that the movement endures for generations to come. Together, we have the power to create a world that is more just, equitable, and compassionate, and it all begins with how we care for ourselves and each other.

About the Author

Fearless Activist and Advocate for Women

Darlene Meissner is a seasoned advocate, activist, and changemaker with over two decades of experience championing women and driving transformational change. Known for her unapologetic confidence and fearless advocacy, Darlene has spent her life breaking down systemic barriers and supporting women and gender diverse folks to reclaim their power and purpose.

With resilient determination, Darlene has helped hundreds of women shed the emotional and societal burdens that hold them back, uncovering their unique strengths and creating lasting change. Her activism goes beyond support—it's about igniting bold shifts that allow women and gender diverse folks to step into their dreams with a renewed sense of confidence and possibility.

A passionate advocate with a background in social work, Darlene brings unwavering energy to every space she occupies, empowering women and gender diverse folks to embrace their professional and personal lives unapologetically. She believes that within everyone lies the power to thrive, and her mission is to help them access it.

Darlene's work is a rallying call for all women and allies to step forward, lighter and stronger, into the lives they've always imagined.

You will find multiple ways to connect with Darlene at https://www.darlenemeissner.com/